GW00985547

Quail Keeping: Beg...........

Raising Quails and Getting Profits

Table Of Contents

Introduction..3

Chapter 1. Having a Good Quail Farming Business Plan 4

Chapter 2. All You Need to Know About Quail Eggs 8

Chapter 3. Taking Care of Your Quail Chicks...13

Chapter 4. Choosing a Quail Breed..16

Chapter 5. Keeping Quails for Commercial Farming..19

Chapter 6. Quail Diseases..23

Chapter 7. Raising Your Quails in a Healthy Manner 27

Conclusion 30

Introduction

I would first like to thank and congratulate you on downloading **"Quail Keeping: Ultimate Guide to Raising "Golden Birds" and Getting Profits."** You will find that raising quails can be a very lucrative business in the poultry farming industry. It is very popular today as a good source of income. You can start your quail farming with just a little capital, and it will give you high returns on investment.

In order to make your quail farming a lucrative one you need to make sure that you are not wasting money on birds that are unhealthy, don't lay eggs and die. In this book you are going to go through the steps you will need to take as a beginner in the quail farming business in order to make a profit at it.

If you handle the running of your quail farming well, you are going to do well in receiving good profits for your efforts. However, you need to learn the steps in what you must do in order to be raising a healthy flock of quails and that is what you will be offered within the pages of this guide book that I have written. I hope that you find much pleasure and success in raising your quails. Just think of how nice it will be to have real fresh eggs literally in your own backyard!

Chapter 1. Having a Good Quail Farming Business Plan

In order for you to breath life into your quail farming business plan you must stick to it religiously. It is a very good idea to have a good solid business plan before you start any business venture. Having a quail farming business plan will help guide you towards running your business at a profit.

A very good idea when first starting out is to visit local quail farms in your area, talk to the farmers, get some advice on how they raise them successfully. You may even have to pay a small fee for this information, but it will be well worth it. You want to raise your quails strong and healthy. If you can find out from local successful quail farmers what their secrets to quail farming success are it would be well worth the fee if one is requested.

When you are writing up your quail farming business plan, you need to make sure that you are clear what exactly is the goal you are looking to reach in it. Ask yourself questions such as the following:

What is the purpose behind your production of quails? Ask yourself right from the beginning what is the reason you have behind keeping quails—for commercial reasons or just to have a source of fresh eggs and meat to provide for your immediate family? Or are you raising them more as a hobby? This is the first step that you need to clarify.

Quail products to produce:

Before you make a decision on what products to produce you need to research and find out what bird's products are popular at the point in time when you are going to start your quail farm. This is valuable information to know when you finally do begin your quail farming.

There is basically four areas that you can choose from:

- Breeding—selling fertilized eggs, day old quail chicks, or a week or two old etc.
- Raising birds for meat and egg production
- Raising for meat production
- Raising for egg production

Housing for your quails:

You will need to provide your quails with safe and secure housing with all the necessary requirements to ensure their health and safety. This will then make them become more productive. You can raise quails in cages or on floors. You need to make sure that the housing they are in is properly ventilated and that they have a fresh supply of water and well balanced feeds.

Hire Laborer:

If you decide to run a large size quail farm you may need to consider hiring a laborer to help you with the running of the quail farm. Quails in general are very easy to manage, this will require minimal help. Of course you can always turn to your own family members to pitch in with the caring of the quails.

Quality of feeds:

The level of quality in the products that you produce from your quails is going to largely depend on the quality of the feeds that you are feeding your quails. Quail birds are known to be fussy eaters, so make sure to provide them with well-balanced feeds, placing in an area where they do not need to strain to gain access to them.

A healthy adult quail can easily consume 30grams of feed per day. You need to make sure that the feeds have a good amount of proteins in them, as the birds require protein in order to produce healthy eggs and to maintain their feathers.

You can feed them turkey or chicken feeds. They consume less feeds compared to other poultry birds such as chickens and turkeys. So when it comes to your capital investment it will be less compared to raising other poultry breeds.

Breeding quails:

A male quail can easily take care of five females a day, for the purposes of breeding it is a good idea to have one male for every three females. Quail females are not very good egg hatchers since becoming domesticated. You will need to invest in a good egg incubator to help you hatch the eggs. That is of course if you are keeping the birds for breeding purposes.

Quail care:

There are a number of diseases that quails are resistant to that effect other poultry birds. They are however, prone to getting infections due to improper care and poor management. If you make an effort to take proper care of your quails you will be protecting them against health-related issues.

Marketing quail products:

You will need to put together a good marketing strategy in order to gain profit from your quail farming. When you have a good strategy for marketing you will be able to sell the quail products that you have produced at good competitive prices.

You need to know what your total cost will be in producing your quail products so that you make your total selling cost higher then your total cost of production.

You can sell your quail eggs in various ways such as going to the local farmer's market in your area, supplying them in crates to local grocery stores, or selling them over the internet. You can also package and brand your quail meat to sell to local stores.

Chapter 2. All You Need to Know About Quail Eggs

Female quails begin to lay eggs at only six weeks old. The female quail can average about 25 eggs in a month, which is 300 eggs, especially the Japanese quails. Now you are getting to know what you will have in store for you when getting into quail farming, so let us look closer into the details of it.

You can choose from several ways to approach starting into quail farming, the most two common ways are either starting with hatching quail eggs that are fertile quail eggs into chicks through incubation of the eggs, or going with live birds (preferably quail chicks) from local breeders or quail farmers. It is vital that you learn how to identify good quail eggs suitable for incubation.

Identifying unsuitable quail eggs for incubation:

 It is a vital part of the incubation process that you know how to tell if the eggs are fertile and suitable for incubation.

You want to possess these skills so you can avoid incubating abnormal and unfertilized eggs which in turn could lead to massive losses of resources and time. You want to operate your quail farming at a profit not at a loss, so this is a vital step in ensuring that you do just that.

It can be a challenge to learn how to tell the difference between a normal/fertile quail egg and one that is abnormal/infertile. It would be so disappointing to you to find at the end of your waiting for your precious quail eggs to hatch only to find that they are abnormal or infertile, this can be a costly mistake in time and money. The list below points out signs for you to look for that will let you know if the eggs are unsuitable for incubation:

* Double yolk
* Very thin eggshells
* Cracks on the eggshell
* Bloody spots on the yolk of the egg, this you can detect through candling

Verifying fertility of incubated quail eggs:

The first step you must take in helping ensure that eggs are fertilized is to make a good pairing of your quails: one male to a maximum of three females is a good number. You can candle the eggs on the seventh day of incubation to see if they are indeed fertile. When you use a candling lamp you will either see a reddish embryo that is a fertile egg, or a clear embryo which is an infertile egg.

If you are not sure about the colors on the seventh day you can wait until the 13th or 14th day of incubation and candle them again at that time. If the chick is absent a larger part of the egg is a clear embryo, but if the chick is present in the egg the embryo will look darker in color, the light may not penetrate it through the eggshell. Make sure you are very careful when you are doing the candling process so you do not damage the eggs.

Incubation

You first need a suitable incubator for your quail eggs, that is going to offer a suitable temperature that is relative to humidity and offers adequate supply of fresh air. You need to turn the eggs 180°, three times within a 24 hour period. Doing this turning step of the eggs is going to help ensure that they are heated evenly, except the last three days of hatching, or day 15 onwards.

Successfully incubating quail eggs:

It will take on the average about 18 to 24 days to hatch quail eggs. There is now mutants of quails that their eggs take an average of 14 to 17 days to hatch. You will probably find that the hatching rate of your quail eggs will be fairly high if you take the proper steps needed to help ensure this. For eggs that are incubated several days and below have a higher chance of hatching. Eggs that are older than ten days have a lower rate of hatching.

To help increase your hatch rate only use eggs that are several days or less in your incubation process. You should make sure to keep the incubator nice and clean and disinfected. The temperatures inside your incubator should range in the area of 99.5° to 100.5° Fahrenheit. Make sure to read the manufacturer's manual of your incubator and read how to best handle your particular brand of incubator.

Put your quail eggs at room temperature for a few hours before putting them inside the incubator. Make sure the eggs are clean, and free from any abnormalities, candle check them. In order for your incubator to provide you with the end result of hatched quail eggs it must be kept at a suitable temperature, have fresh air and relative humidity.

If your incubator is a manual one you must remember to turn your eggs three times within a 24 hour period to make sure that the heat is evenly dispersed over your eggs. Next we will look into poor egg-hatch and the solutions for each cause. Below are six of the leading causes of poor egg hatch and the solutions for them:

- **Incubating infertile eggs:** It can be most disappointing when you are waiting and waiting with high hopes of your quail eggs hatching only to find that they are infertile quail eggs.

Solution: You need to make sure to candle your quail eggs before and during the incubation process (before the 15th day to help you to detect any infertile eggs. You also need to pair your quails properly, one male to three females to help ensure that the eggs will be fertilized.

- **Incubating abnormal/defective eggs:** If the egg has cracks, double yolk, absence of yolk, or dark bloody spots it will be considered to be defective.

Solution: You need to candle your eggs before you incubate them, so that abnormal

eggs are not taking up space inside your incubator.

Make sure that you are collecting your quail eggs at least two times per day, store your quail eggs in a humid room with pointy end facing upwards.

- **Failure to turn incubated eggs:** You turn your eggs to ensure that your eggs are evenly warmed. If you fail to do this you can run the risk of overheating one area of your egg/this will make it unsuitable for hatching chicks.

Solution: When you are in the incubating process make sure that you are turning your quail eggs at least three times every twenty-four hours. You can also use an automatic egg incubator which has the ability to turn the eggs to the 180° angle three time a day.

- **Conditions of incubator are unfavourable:** You need to make sure that there is the proper amount of fresh air, suitable temperatures, and relative humidity so that your quail eggs can hatch.

Solution: Choose an incubator that has the ability to hatch eggs. You need to make sure that you clean and disinfect your incubator before use. If you have power failures often in your area it would be a worth while investment to have some kind of power backup.

- **Eggs looked like they were fertile but still did not hatch:** This may happen if you are incubating eggs from older quail breeds. It could also be caused by waiting too long after the eggs were laid to put into the incubator.

Solution: Incubate eggs from pairs of young quails. Choose eggs that are seven days or less old. You do not want to hold eggs in your holding facility for more than eight days as this will lessen the chances of the eggs hatching. Do not wash any dirty eggs, this can cause the natural protective layer on the egg to be washed off, exposing entry by organisms, hampering the ability of you being able to hatch quail eggs successfully.

- **Not managing egg incubator well:** If you are not managing the temperatures and humidity properly in your incubator this could result in your eggs not hatching. If your incubator is unclean this too can result in poor hatching results.

Solution: Make sure that you have got the right temperatures and humidity during incubation process. Keep your incubator in a room that the temperature does not fluctuate and that allows humidity to occur. Make sure that you clean and disinfect before using it.

Chapter 3. Taking Care of Your Quail Chicks

Your quail chicks will take about 18-24 days to hatch on average from an egg that has been successfully incubated. When your quail eggs hatch you 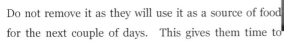 may see that the chicks have an attachment of egg yolk on their abdomen.

Do not remove it as they will use it as a source of food for the next couple of days. This gives them time to adjust to their new lifestyle outside of the egg. Do not be concerned that the chicks are tiny, they will have the ability to feed themselves. You do need to keep in mind that they are very sensitive to cold and hot temperatures. To avoid your chicks from drowning in the water troughs fill them half-way with small marbles.

There are two ways that you can acquire quail chicks: getting them from a local quail breeder or farmer, or go through the incubation process and successfully incubate your own eggs. After the chicks have hatched you will then transfer them to a brooder. Below are some tips to what a good brooder should consist of.

Source of heat: You need this in order to keep the temperatures regulated inside of your brooder. You may use heat sources such as heat lamps, charcoal burners or gas burners. The brooder needs to be heated properly.

The two best ways for you to make sure of this is to use a thermometer or keep close observation on the behavior that your chicks are doing around the heating source. If the chicks are crowding around the heat source this is a sure sign that there is cold in the brooder somewhere getting in. When you see the chicks staying far away from the heating source this means that the heat is too high.

When you have reached a nice temperature within your brooder the chicks should be evenly dispersed around the brooder. You should work at maintaining a temperature of 95° Fahrenheit during the first week.

After that it should be lowered by five degrees on each passing week until the fourth week when they are ready to be taken out of the brooder. You should be able to withdraw the source of heat by the fourth week, this will allow the birds to adapt to their surroundings.

Litter: Litter helps to keep your brooder warm by absorbing wet moisture. You may get litter in the form of wood shavings or sawdust. Litter that has been used needs to be discarded from your brooder to avoid spillage of any undesired odor from the brooder to the other surroundings.

Feeders: You need to place nice and clean feeders at convenient spots where your chicks are not straining to access them. The feeders need to be made in such a way so that the chicks cannot defecate in them.

You should make sure that you have well-balanced feeds available for your quail chicks at all times. You can feed your quails on game bird feeds or turkey feeds a starter feed that has an average of 25% protein.

Once your quails are four-weeks old you should change their feed to layers mash. Since your quails will begin laying eggs at six weeks, it is a good idea to change to mash as your quails reach egg laying stage.

Correct amount of light: You need to make sure that your brooder is correctly lit so the chicks can see the feeds and water source. For a small size operation a bulb can serve well as the light source for a brooder. You can also use a heating bulb in your housing area for chicks eight days old or below. This will serve as both a source of heat and light for your quail chicks. Infrared lights will not disturb the sleeping patterns of your chicks inside the brooder.

Proper ventilation: There should be a proper amount of fresh air in the brooder. This is vital to allow for gaseous exchange and to keep the respiratory-related infections out of your brooder.

Waterers: The quail waterers should be designed in such a way cannot step into or defecate in them. You should have plenty of drinking water made available to your quails. You need to make sure that the water supply is clean and is located in a spot that is not going to have your quails stressed out. One of the leading causes of mortality in quail chicks is that they drown in waterers. So remember to put in the marbles to help ensure the safety of your quail chicks. You should clean the waterers on a daily basis, after about three weeks remove the marbles.

Note: The location of your brooder should be away from any sources of noise and disturbance to your quail chicks. It should be a secure area for your quail chicks that will keep them protected. Raise your quail chicks under good sanitary conditions and you should be running at a profit in your quail farming venture in no time

!

Chapter 4. Choosing a Quail Breed

If you begin your quail farming with a desirable breed you can expect a desirable output. Depending on what your purpose is behind keeping quails will largely help to determine the type of quail breed you should go with. People keep different quail breeds for different reasons.   Reasons differ from keeping for their meat, eggs or for both, or simple as domestic pets.

Different quail breeds have different personalities. You need to decide and do some research into the type of personality that you are interested in your quails exhibiting. Go to your local quail farmers to find out more about the personalities of the different breeds and the production capabilities of them.

When starting out with quail farmer it is best to choose a local breed that will be readily available to you. Depending on the type of breed of quail that you choose to go with will determine the kinds of financial gains you will receive from your quail farming.

You need to put some special effort when you make your choice of what your initial flock of quail breed will be. The steps below will help guide you in making sure that you make a good decision in your first flock of quails.

* Find out if there is licensed quail farmers in your area. These are the people that you

need to look into and decide who you shall go with when purchasing your first flock. Aim to gain the best performing breeds from the local quail farmers.

- You should make a point of visiting at least three different quail farmers to see how each of them goes about raising their quails, and the types of quail breeds they are raising and why. Find out what the capabilities of the different breeds are.

- Do not buy a flock that has birds that are different colors or have deformaties, or are different sizes. If they are different sizes this will cause them to fight more, resulting in low unprofitable outputs.

- You need to stick to one type of quail breed. Avoid mixing quail breeds as they may end up fighting with each other.

- Find out what the history of mortality or diseases of the different breeds are that you are considering purchasing. Most breeders have records of this in their possession.

- If you decide you want to buy eggs then make sure that the eggs have no abnormalities.

How to tell the difference between the male and female quail:

If you are planning to raise quails for egg or meat production you need to know how to tell the difference between the two sexes. If you decide that you want to begin raising quails for egg or meat production you need to know how to tell the difference between the sexes.

You would not want to find yourself raising all males quails hoping for eggs to be laid—you could be waiting a long long time for that miracle to happen. Or don't raise female quails without expecting them to lay eggs. Below I have listed things to look out for when identifying if a quail is male or female.

- **Looking at the physical appearance:** When female quails have reached maturity they will look bigger in size than the males of the same breed and age.

- **Examine the quail's vent/cloacae:** This is one on of the best ways to distinguish a female quail from a male quail. There are two different ways that you can examine the vent. First you can press the area around it with two fingers, if a ball-like lump pops forward this suggests the bird is male. If there is not ball-like lump then this will suggest to you that the quail if female. Also when you press the vent and some white foam comes out of it then this too would suggest that it is a male quail. If there is no foam then it would suggest that the bird is a female.

- **Roosting of your quails:** When male quails are about five weeks several will begin to roost (they begin making soft noise). You can also use the roosting to tell the male from the female. It is only the male birds that roost.

- **Check pattern of quail's chest:** The female quails have speckled feathers on their chests while the male quails have plain chest feathers. This method will only work on quails that have grown enough feathers; usually about three weeks old and onwards.

Chapter 5. Keeping Quails for Commercial Farming

It is very common knowledge within the poultry industry that quail farming requires very little investment but will offer you great returns. People starting into or considering getting into quail farming wonder if keeping quails can really be profitable! The truth of the matter is it can be a real dream or it could end up being a real nightmare for you this of course will depend greatly on how you approach quail farming.

If you start out with the right breed of quails and proper housing, in a suitable environment, feeding them the proper feeds and clean water supply, are is minimal chance that you will fail at quail farming. However, if you start off with the wrong kind of breeds, wrong housing, wrong feeds, and failure to provide the quails with a safe and sanitary living environment then you are basically setting yourself up for failure.

Raising quails is great in that you do not need a lot of capital investment to get yourself started into quail farming. And the fact that it offers great returns sounds like a win win situation if you follow the proper procedures when raising them.

Due to the low capital investment in quail farming and great returns quail farming has become popular all over the world. Are you aware that if you start off with just fifty birds and in two or three years, you could be taking in millions from your investment? The trick to succeed well is to invest the profits of the first year or two back into your quail farm, and after that you are going to reap major profits from this venture.

You need to do your research into finding out what you need to produce to maximize your profits, and take action to make sure that the necessary steps are taken to put your plan into action. You really can't go wrong in quail farming if you focus on production of eggs and chicks. Below I have put together a list of the products and byproducts of quail farming. You must make a decision what are the products that you want to focus on producing on your quail farming project.

- **Unfertilized eggs:** You can raise female quails that are isolated from males and they will eventually lay unfertilized eggs once they are of egg laying age. When there is no mating between the male and female quails this will result in unfertilized eggs. Producing unfertilized eggs is a common commercial trend with quail farmers.

  You will find quail eggs being sold at local farmer's markets, and grocery stores. Quail eggs are consumed by many people across the globe. They have been scientifically proven to contain many health and medicinal benefits, making them a popular meal choice by many.

- **Fertilized eggs:** When you have your male and female quails together the female will produce fertilized eggs. The fertilized eggs have the chance of hatching into chicks. To help ensure that the eggs are being fertilized pair one male with two to three hens.

- **Quail chicks:** After the incubation period is completed successfully, the fertilized eggs will hatch into chicks. You need to be organized and have customers set up that are interested in acquiring the chicks at a few days old. People that want chicks want to acquire them at a few days old when they are raising them.

- **Point of lay quail birds:** These are female quails from the age of six weeks onwards. These are the female quails that are at the egg laying stage. When your chicks hatch you need to take care of them by providing them with well-balanced feed, medications, and fresh water supply. This will help to ensure that they will reach the point of lay healthy and productive for a long period of time.

- **Manure:** the waste matter of quails is a useful by-product for farming purposes. Quail's droppings are organic in nature with high levels of nitrogen. Many crop farmers are looking for it all over the world to spread over their fields.

- **Meat:** You may choose to raise broilers specifically for meat production, or you may decide to have some layers and some broilers. When female quails stop laying they are then often slaughtered for their meat. You can pack and freeze quail meat to be sold at grocery stores and restaurants. You can even smoke the meat for special order types. They have a nice taste and can stay preserved for a long time.

You do not have to buy already egg-laying female quails

It is not easy to tell the age of a female that is already laying eggs. You may want to purchase quails that are just ready to be going into their age laying stage or may have recently just started into it. Or you can raise your quails from chicks.

Quails will slow down and put on weight as they approach the full maturity stage. It has been found that female quails lay eggs consistently through the first couple of years of their egg laying stage. In the later years their egg laying may slow down or will stop altogether as they age. Female quails at the age of four onwards are more likely to lay eggs that are infertile. This could lead to massive loss if the farmer is not careful if he is hoping these birds will give him fertilized eggs for incubation.

If you have decided that you are going to raise quails for commercial egg production then I would suggest that you choose utmost five week old quails. At that stage their vitality and productiveness will then be guaranteed. However you may choose to hatch your own fertilized eggs, then that would be the best option.

Chapter 6. Quail Diseases

Quails overall are a very hardy bird that resistant to many diseases that are other poultry birds. If you are just basic quail farming operation you are to have the equipment or know-how on detect quail diseases or diagnose them have some sort of training. It will of very challenging to diagnose internal in your quails.  a r e affecting running a not going h o w t o unless you course be infections

There is lots of ongoing research being done on diseases that affect quails. Hopefully this will help the future quail farmers in gaining more extensive knowledge on dealing with the common diseases of quails. I have listed below four common quail diseases and their preventions and treatments.

- **Coccidiosis:** Coccidiosis is a parasitic infection which can effect the digestive tracts, usually with quails over seven weeks of age are resistant to Coccidiosis, but birds under seven weeks it is more severe in its impact. What happens is the birds that are infected will slow down and stop eating. If they are not treated in time they will most likely die.

- **Prevention and Treatment:** This disease is usually due to poor management of farms, not keeping the poultry house clean and dry. Coccidiosis mainly thrives in areas where there is a build up of quail droppings. You need to make sure that your quail cages are kept dry and free of built-up quail droppings. You can also get feeds that are laced with a drug called coccidiostat; this drug will help to prevent infection by Coccidiosis. The birds eating this type of feed will build up an immunity against the disease.

- **Worms/Thread Worms/Crop Worms:** Another parasite that affects quails is worms. The most dangerous are the worms that infect the lining of the bird's crop. The infection of crop worms can not be diagnosed just by looking at your quail. The infected crop had to be opened and then worms can be seen in their thread-like appearance in the lining of the tissue on the bird's crop. Bird's that are infected can eat a lot but look like they are starving. In the later stages of this infection the birds have a hard time breathing. These are the two most common physical symptoms of this ailment.

Prevention and Treatment: Thread worms or crop worms thrive in wet droppings and wet areas in and around the feeders. The best way to prevent the spread of these worms is to build the base of your bird cages with wire mesh. The spaces within the mesh would not allow the build-up of wet droppings to occur. You need to make sure the cages are raised off the ground, maybe have a catch tray below them for catching the droppings. Use a proper de-wormer to treat these crop worms. Ask your local vet for the best treatment for this in your area.

- **Ulcerative Enteritis:** Ulcerative enteritis is another quail bird disease that is destructive. The disease shows up on the inside of the internal linings of the infected bird's intestines. The best way to diagnose this is to do lab tests. This can also be transmitted from one bird to the other through contact with droppings of infected bird. The birds that recover from this are usually the disease carriers.

Prevention and Treatment: The best thing that you can do to help ensure that there is not a spread of this fatal disease is to take measures to ensure that your quail cages are kept in a sanitary condition. If one bird appears infected take measures to quarantine it from the rest of the flock until you can determine what the diagnosis reveals.

- **Histomoniasis:** This is one of the most lethal diseases that can affect your quails. This disease is also known as blackhead. It is a protozoan infection that is known to attack a number of poultry breeds. It is usually a disease found in the larger foul unit. Histomoniasis infects the quail's liver and starts to immediately produce necrotic lesions which result in fatal liver damage to the quails. Birds that are infected with this may seem to appear very restless, have a poor appetite, loss of feathers and sulfur-colored droppings.

Prevention and Treatment: It is believed that the birds that recover from histomoniasis are the carriers of the disease. Avoid mixing chickens with quails. You should use de-wormers, to help eliminate the cecal worms which transmit histomoniasis. There has yet to be found an effective treatment for this, but the best thing you can do is to take preventative measure by not mixing your quails amongst chickens.

Signs that a quail is sick:

- **Unresponsive, numb:** Quails that are sick will appear numb and unresponsive. They will often be seen sleeping on the floor of their housing. When standing they may have an abnormal posture.

- **Lack of appetite:** When quails are sick they will lack a normal healthy appetite, consume less quantities of feeds compared to what a healthy quail would consume.

- **Plumage:** If your quails have feathers that are falling out or appear rough in their appearance and texture check the quail for infection.

- **Difficulty in breathing:**   If your quail has blocked mucus membranes or any observable or hearable sound indicating that they are having trouble breathing this is a sign that they could have a respiratory infection, possibly pneumonia.

- **Weight loss:** A quail that is ill may lose their appetite and will begin to lose weight and dehydrate.

- **Observable defects in defecations:** If your quail's defecation is blood stained this is a sign that there is some kind of internal infection. If there is worms in it then that is a parasitic infection. If it is very watery this is a sign that it has diarrhea or if it is hard it is a sign that the quail if dehydrated.

- **Lack of interest or listless behavior:** If you have a quail that seems to have no interest even when you present it with good quality feed it may be ill.

- **Reduction of productivity:** If you notice a sudden reduction in the amount of eggs that your quail flock is producing this could be a sign that there is an infection within your flock of quails.

- **Very low or high temperatures:** If your quails temperature is too high or too low it may be a sign that the quail in not well.

Chapter 7. Raising Your Quails in a Healthy Manner

When you manage to keep your quails well fed, living in safe
and sanitary housing, keeping them in a state of good healthy
by making sure all is functioning well with them you will reap
the benefits of your efforts. Below I have listed several reasons
why it is important that you keep your flock of quails healthy:

- To produce quality eggs and meat products. You want to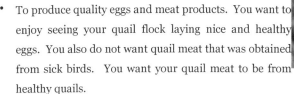
  enjoy seeing your quail flock laying nice and healthy
  eggs. You also do not want quail meat that was obtained
  from sick birds. You want your quail meat to be from
  healthy quails.

- When your quails are in good health they will not be spreading any contagious
  diseases among the flock or to humans for that matter.

- Healthy quails mature fast and are vibrant and have a longer lifespan. They are
  generally found to have high productivity.

- When you raise healthy quails they are cost-effective to raise. You will not have a lot of
  bills regarding treatments.

- Quails that are healthy are going to give you a higher market value than unhealthy
  quails.

Below are the essentials you will need to raise yourself a flock of healthy quails:

- Make sure that you are well-informed about the raising of quails. Know exactly what you are getting into it is well worth the research. Be informed in what the latest develops in quail farming are.

- Depending on your purpose for your quails make sure that you choose a suitable breed for your needs. If you start with a popular desirable breed then you can expect to have a desirable output.

- Make sure that you are going to provide your flock of quails with the proper housing facility or space for quails to be safely reared in, depending on your choice of breed.

- Know about the different kinds of feeds for quail and learn how to perform basic disease management steps during the rearing of your quail flock. Go and ask professional quail farmers for tips on how to get started in your area in quail farming.

- It is a good idea to give your quail flock some exposure to sunlight. Your quails need the vitamin D just as you do from the sunlight.

- Make sure that you provide your quail flock with well-balanced feeds and clean fresh drinking water at room temperature.

- Provide grit for your flock to help aid in food digestion.

- Supply your quail with fresh greens, to supplement their feeds. Hang these in their cages to keep them busy pecking at them.

- Good sanitation and grooming is vital. You must keep your quails in a clean environment. This I cannot stress enough, the best way to keep diseases at bay is to keep your quail flock in a clean housing area. You need to be able to handle the birds properly while giving vaccinations. Or culling the flock.

- Use correct disinfectants to use on the cages, waterers, feeders.

- Offer your quail flock a nice peaceful environment to thrive in. They do not like noisy surroundings and can remain unproductive in noisy surroundings.

Basically what it all boils down to is that if you provide your quails with a safe and clean environment to live accompanied with healthy food and clean water you are going to be rewarded with healthy good quality sources of fresh eggs and quail meat. You need to focus on raising healthy quails and in return you will make a healthy profit!

Conclusion

I hope that you will find my guide book as a beginner in quail farming both insightful and informative in helping you to get yourself up and started into this lucrative business of quail farming.

I would strongly suggest that you go to a couple of local quail farmers and gain as much insight and information from them that you can on the best way to start in your area in quail farming. Ask them what the best breeds of quail are in your area to raise. You can gain from their experience in the raising of quails. The more prepared you are the higher the chances are that you will succeed in your quail farming business.

I would like to thank you once again for downloading my book, I would really appreciate if you could take a moment to write a short review of my book on Amazon. Thanks so much for your kind support of my work! Best of luck on your new venture into quail farming!

FREE Bonus Reminder

If you have not grabbed it yet, please go ahead and download your special bonus report *"DIY Projects. 13 Useful & Easy To Make DIY Projects To Save Money & Improve Your Home!"*
Simply Click the Button Below

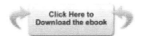

OR **Go to This Page**
http://diyhomecraft.com/free

BONUS #2: More Free & Discounted Books

Do you want to receive more Free & Discounted Books?

We have a mailing list where we send out our new Books when they go free or with a discount on Kindle. Click on the link below to sign up for Free & Discount Book Promotions.

=> Sign Up for Free & Discount Book Promotions <=

OR Go to this URL

http://zbit.ly/1WBb1Ek

Printed in Great Britain
by Amazon